Lachlan Brown | Lunar Inheritance

New Poems

GIRAMONDO POETS

Lachlan Brown | Lunar Inheritance

First published 2017
from the Writing & Society Research Centre
at the University of Western Sydney
by the Giramondo Publishing Company
PO Box 752 Artarmon NSW 1570 Australia
www.giramondopublishing.com

Designed by Harry Williamson
Typeset by Andrew Davies
in 10/16.5 pt Baskerville BT

Printed and bound by Ligare
Distributed in Australia by NewSouth Books

National Library of Australia
Cataloguing-in-Publication data:

Brown, Lachlan –
Lunar inheritance / Lachlan Brown
ISBN 978-1-925336-38-2 (pbk)
A821.4

For my mother, Pauline Brown, with gratitude and tears

'Do not lay up for yourselves treasures on earth,
where moth and rust destroy
and where thieves break in and steal.'

MATTHEW 6:19

'In Beijing as well as in Gwanjiu and Berlin, it evoked strong responses from the audience, some of whom wept in front of it as if encountering a long lost friend or relative.'

WU HUNG, 'ABOUT *WASTE NOT*:
THINGS, MEMORY, AND FAMILY ETHICS'

'what's the use writing poetry
in this ancient city
since the new era has arrived'

YI SHA, 'THE ANCIENT CITY'

Contents

1 Sanctioned entry
7 Position repossession
13 Chinese Container
15 Self-storage
21 Crispy buildings in many different settings
27 The menu at Macquarie Fields Chinese Restaurant
29 Viewfind
35 Becoming a small capitalist
41 Tell it like it is
43 Blend
49 The benefits of civic living
55 Filling out a Form
57 So much that we have lost and cannot hope to regain
63 Stick with your group
69 Artistic Licenses
71 Blank face double vision
77 Almost there

84 Notes
86 Acknowledgements

Sanctioned entry

(a future for each object)
Guangzhou approach and buildings
seen from the air become Mahjong tiles
neatly stacked by your grandfather's
imagined hands as he meets with the clan
back on Dixon street, Sydney, and this may be
the last time you will see cleansky
for the clouds are breathed memories
and you finally fall beneath them.

(safe break)
Silent highways   therefore the driver
flicks his high beams in   a kind of
urgent   morse code and each gap
in the traffic is either   a dot   or a dash
but you   can't keep track of it all because
even one   wrong letter is the difference
between construction   and constriction
in Guangzhou's knotted   city centre.

(revenant opiate)
Double-edged grace,
your cousins auditing the world,
the dishes your mother never let you choose,
the smack addict in Cabramatta's gleaming sunshine,
your cousins crossing Border Leicesters alongside the Lachlan,
unsettled wool prices like a seismograph gone haywire,
short selling all these rapturous futures,
gerrymandering electorates in the shape of sheepyards.

(the path of reform)
Brave CNJOY Mall stands on the bronze shoulders
of the statues in Martyrs' Park demonstrating
that the people now have hope and H&M
and levels of jackets with price tags that
flash like the white teeth of the sharks
in tanks on the top floor swimming
their eerie laps as though time's
moebius strip could be reversed.

(top of the city)
Bags of children's clothing, hundreds of used McDonalds cups,
    a sign that reads 'Free to a Good Home': these things
take up residence in your grandmother's four-bedroom house
    surrounding her like the untruths she repeats in set patterns,
looping her stories like a sentry's pathway through a Shanghai gated
    community. When the lies eventually displace her body
she finds sleep in a backyard shed listening to Sydney's thin rain
    and rats chewing through bundles of forgotten currency.

(titulus)
Skip ahead to reconditioned ethnicity,
phlegm's supremacy, the streaked pavement
an icon for these next few decades, introducing
aspirational living where everybody gets a car.
Think of a number, double it, look under your seat,
subtract the number you originally thought of.
Policy's ambitious ambit knows all answers,
begins to draft a contract for our expanding universe.

(miscegenate this)
The weird glances your family gets
in the Hurstville BBQ restaurant
as though the word had finally
become Hainan chicken-flesh
and was now dwelling among us.
You figure it's because of your dad,
the only white guy in the place, his joyous fork
dividing joints and marrow, tendons and tripe.

(new lucky four eyes: for the director of music)
Re-engaged by a noble refusal
cinching culture and identity:
the kite string on the New
Year's parade float which you
sense will somehow still electro-
cute you whether this weather
changes or not (the cat waving
its arm like a frenzied conductor).

Position repossession

(fathersong)

In Yuexiu Park I imagine my past
strung out like those red lanterns along curved stone paths.
A man swings a sword in the shifting light
and it circumnavigates the lake, returning in an instant.
Suddenly I want to ask that man to send his sword
to visit my son in Australia.
'He is blond-haired and one quarter Chinese' I want to say,
but I cannot speak the language of the Guangzhou morning.

(overseas Chinese are the mother of revolution)

Sun Yat-sen is framed   by Guangzhou skyscrapers
his metallic figure rewriting   the poem your grand-
mother proudly   recited in Cantonese before you left
Sydney, and you   recall too the Sun Yat-sen medallion
you discovered   in the eighth month of the first year
of cleaning her Ashfield   house, and her pained features as you
smashed a broken metal   chair on the road right in front
of her, its diasporic   pieces like shards of shining guilt.

(nostalgia for some impartial hierarchies of living)
Life's no longer the thing we thought, for it is
impossible to match words with their objects.
This occurs because certain objects proliferate;
they are gathered into rooms that house many other objects.
So we are filling and refilling dumpsters with objects,
we are speaking only of objects,
we are dreaming of unnamed objects pursuing us
through this plastic-bagged matrushka-dolled existence.

(in youth mode, you are infinite)
Start acting basic.
Start thinking of yourself as a street photographer.
Start digging up the pavement in the square
beneath the drum and bell towers.
Start preparing for disruptive technologies.
Start living your life
as though it were a tower defence game
(next wave approaching).

(remainders in two parts of the same world)

In the wet Beijing road refracts its own light
leans in on itself so there's no way   you
can ever walk straight. The update mall experience
is itself a recursion   of all experience
so you stay out late   waiting until things begin
to close   trying hard to catch
commerce   shutting itself down
winding security grilles over your head.

(curriculum vitae)

Banyan trees with limbs
crosshatching whole apartment blocks,
            the sky's sketched edges
                 rapidly darkening,
and a day already
            performance-reviewing itself,
with birds retrospectively true,
       just perching there in point form.

(vox populi)
Around the world ((y)our) people begin to wake
and someone jokes and tells me to go back to coaching college.
How do you resuscitate the traditions of a selective school?
We imagine huge losses in the rugby comp. We see a sign
for South China Power Creative Science Park. And our hidden
fears pile up like those precariously balanced carcasses
of smashed cars in a large field, meaning that there's no space
for high ground, just ghostly backdoors in the wrecker's hardware.

(saving second face)
My mother stacks rice cookers behind
the couch so that she is ready for any gift
emergency.   She learned to cook Chinese
food from books, recuperating her authenticity
with the same vigour as the slap of peanut
oil hitting a scorching wok.   The night before
I leave home I ask her to teach me to cook
and her eyes widen in disbelief.

Chinese Container

Always the bewildered face, the recalcitrant hair
no barber can resolve (and so you just envision
yourself without it). Your veins are a river system,
generations in the masking. Names flow out in prayer

or just evaporate into the globally-warmed air,
while you catch your manufactured breath. Transition-
al arrangements seem to always be in place, so listen
to each election result with the utmost care.

Who prayed for a double portion of the Spirit?
Who knows the word beyond the horizon's words?
Two migrating birds fly through this hazy atmosphere

calling out in a dialect we cannot ever inherit.
They notice us, and fly on, through distant suburbs
where they must learn to observe as well as hear.

Self-storage

(near-sighted)
Another day where the AQI blesses the landscape
with sky as white as a Chinese model's white skin.
The highway is strung beneath redemptive powerlines
as your car skims the country of someone's blood, and this
flight mode vision means that you can know nothing
truly   except for the turn-off for Lecong furniture city
        except for a field strewn with broken pots
except for a China Shipping container heading to the coast.

(uncommon denominators)
When she got to Australia in '42 your
grandmother gave herself the western name Sheila,
because that's what the Aussies called her.
Your grandfather chose Allen after the brand of sweets
sold in his mixed business.   Now every tourist
shop offers to write your name in Chinese but no-one
can pronounce it in English and the Australian Embassy
publishes 'porfessor' on the Writers' Week program.

(grandmothercountry)
First night in Kaiping centre and China repeats itself.
The same HK chain stores sit over Bruce Lee's Kung-
fu eatery, which is roundhouse kicking a KFC where
the patrons are rammed in like the chickens they must
now eat. But hey that's capitalism's iterative power
isn't it? KTV soteriology is one price of poverty red-
uction and hence tone-deaf singers find passion in
small rooms echoed by a chorus of moped alarms.

(sorites and another traveller's song)
You won't forget the room of clothes,
piles rising to fill even those upper corners
like light in a Sydney summer. You sense other lives,
your imagined family members,   sizes for those
who will never exist.   The future has its own desert seas,
waves whipping back against a hoarder's precaution
spilling tracksuited ghosts into this bargain bin present.
They whisper the house alive   cursing all dreams.

(life-hyphen)

The way you don't know (what) you are in Austral-
ia until someone yells out 'Fucken gook' from the
bus window is the way you don't notice the Guang-
zhou rain falling until you look up and it has slick-
ed over everything and you find your skin wet and
trembling but the light's polished grey modulations
mean people stop double-taking at your distortion-
pedal face just long enough for you to get past them.

(instant vantage)

The camera can't quite catch it though
your brain sets its oriental filters with
the kind of paratactical manoeuvring
that may offer a defense like those holes
in the dialou balconies meant for shooting
bandits and protecting villages but these Chinese
buildings with western additions – turrets, domes,
composite orders – become your selfied face in reverse.

(signa orientalem)
When my grandmother tells me that she only received
three years of schooling in Wai Long Li she also adds
that she secretly listened to the classroom next door
in order to learn more before she was sent to work forever.
And so from this Kaiping hotel room every murmur of traffic
becomes a poem memorised through village walls
or a snippet of my mother's Latin major reaching out
from the past and somehow proving the West right.

(on Shamian island)
Life of breath O breath of life: birdcall,
ancient trees, quiet traffic across the water,
the exquisite scars of colonial architecture.
Is this moment a small delegation from
the future, the breeze of new creation cutting
back across the face of things, a strange
ambassador in the teeming city that desires
a Kaiping billboard's photoshopped blue skies?

Crispy buildings in many different settings

(four square lives)
You face your old faces in another crowd and soon
after this empty moment you will send back a photo
but your colleagues will tell you the upload stalled,
and so your China-self is a strip of hair against
nondescript buildings. So you now know the reticulated
pattern of a Zili village like those gridbooks where your
friends all practised their Mandarin Saturday characters
while you pressed space bar to jump through traffic.

(as for me)
This house you've cleaned for a year now mother,
you've been cleaning it all your life. We know that
in your tears. On hard days we search the piles
for empathy and finally, when every bin is overflowing,
we realise the poets were right, we can connect nothing
with nothing, because there isn't a story for this material;
there is just nothing following us home in the darkness
whispering 'it's all made in China, made in China, made in…'

(cached psalm)
Massive multiplayer online cosmopolitan city
with every detail Nora Ephronned in advance
like a genial DVD commentary where trucks wear
down distant freeways, or a jazz saxophonist's
ribbon melody winding around infrastructure.
You send me all this: sparrows sold for a few fen,
factories where jeans are hand-cut from the denim sky,
your double-portioned spirit I can no longer flee from.

(Jingjianli metatext)
Official brochure aspect
with front matter like a visa category
that contains every other category.
My un-heritage stacked five
stories high, then a back garden
where a gentle man is keeping bees.
They hum like my grandfather's voice
stirring the elms from some limitless past.

(factical manufacturing)
What you inherit is no ancestral village   with that clotted
overcapacity to emotionally   resonate when the word
'homecoming' is   spoken aloud for the cameras, and what
you inherit is   incredulity toward those crackers splitting
graves   on the hillsides and the voices of families spilling
        down into the valley. But you have not come to an earthly
    city and maybe your name can be written in new characters
evaporating   from summer's pavements.

(a capable range of answers)
When I find my great-grandfather's
naturalisation certificate behind a picture at Ashfield
its information is stripped back, betraying little.
    place and date of birth: Canton, China. 23rd November, 1897.
    colour of eyes: brown
    colour of hair: black
    visible distinguishing marks: nil
Only his signature is a winding blue, like the Tanjiang river
    twisting our distances.

(pride)
Switch off face-recognition
when your mother cries out
after being abused in the street.
Just get to a stage where it's all expected,
for example, at cocktail parties where
even the glasses adjectivise you, because
wealth's a dog-whistling politician building
a platform on graduated levels of hatred.

(vision in a Guangzhou wet market)
Discontinuous schedule:
your skeuomorphic watch relics itself,
winds back nothing
weaponises everything.
Live chickens calling from cages
like a chorus in a tragedy.
Your great-grandmother's cleaver wiped clean
after cutting a neck in her apartment kitchen.

The menu at Macquarie Fields Chinese Restaurant

We're always thinking more or less of Asia:
your eyes like seals on a Chinese scroll
your foreigner's skin and lack of control
(your dumb preference for self-erasure).

This century's about the enclosure
of the ea(s)tery, the splitting of online vitriol
between various revenue streams. Fold
your heritage lovingly, maintain composure.

Remember that here at Peter's Chinese
Restaurant and Personal Computer Repairs
someone's always ordering the Ch'en plain

Chicken. It's our famous special, like these
hard drives wiped as clean as red plastic chairs.
So order a meal, double your RAM, come again.

Viewfind

(some introduction required)
You step off the plane in Shanghai
and vomit   into your sleeve which
is no way   to greet the past or future,
with time running on like that stream of passengers
passing your   inert body, now keeled over
in the airbridge.   And then, when your wheeled
suitcase   somehow carries you down Nanjing Rd
like a hospital gurney, you find the city's voice inside your own.

(absorption method)
The river the colour of a bad espresso
the writer disappears and sentiment doesn't change
the 'n' in Vanguard is upside down
the shape of the claim in the South China Sea
the structure of the speech I leave back at the hotel
the year of the shod horse
the metal detectors at every entrance
emptying pockets of their sharpened words.

(Chinese relations)
Self-censored   emptiness   is the standard I play
on level 38   of the hotel   where capital stretches
the view built by   imported iron awe,   while back
home my family history   aggregates in pools of sweat
on a Western Sydney night,   my mother screaming
at an adopted male phantasm   and my grandmother
mourning her son   and my great-grandmother holding
death like a surrogate child   posing for a photograph.

('11 arrested for leaking exam questions')
Gaokao scalar crowdsourced
attention spans the river created
by the bridge that crosses it.
More proofs for congruence
than you can ever verify
in the assigned code, so just
gamify everything, you islands
give ear to me via these illicit means.

(false prolixity and the diagnostic prophecy)
When my grandmother visits she tells the family
that our lounge room wall good luck characters
are all hanging upside down. Though I'm just a kid
who's still inverting calculators to spell stuff, whilst
each overcompensating generation swings way too far
like an equation for simple-harmonic motion gone wrong.
So now we're unable to say anything in words that matter,
and life's walkthrough proof-texts itself with weird surety.

(new new Shanghai)
Calligraphic skyline, the rise and fall of the Hang Seng
tracked against the ripples on the Huangpu river,
the sun a slow moving barge pushing through
the haze. But you are out of place here above
the internet and the People's Government
and massive overpasses like fat basslines grooving
hard with pentatonic cars, past buildings
elevating development with their silent eyes.

(terminus ante quem)
I am silent before the Liwan tree still growing strong,
before the Chinese government who have increased
military spending by 12.2%, before my mother's de-
termined escape from the prospect of an arranged
marriage, before a picture of Dennis Rodman smoking
cigars and coaching the North Korean basketball
team, before an ocean of my ancestors whose double-
helixed existence necessitates this setting out and return.

(the sediment of low expectations)
auto-capitalisation
in every family line
except this one, where
you miss clanned-out
western destiny like
a modified hatchback
reselling itself in a more
respectable suburb.

Becoming a small capitalist

(wall of frozen dumplings)
This serpent-ribbon, sliding across
the landscape's body, is actually
nothing like the refrigerated
corridors of our century's
hidden desires, patching
logistic-hygiene sensors
into a non-existent grid
on a warming planet.

·

(projected growth)
We clear the yard and discover the Kikuyu grass
  threading its way through mattress after mattress
    like the routes of those who are always leaving Canton
  in the mind's repeated/repeating museum exhibition.
And this just reminds us that we are not special,
  that we exist somewhere along the split ganglion of displaced
    peoples. Yet those fingers in the grass won't release their grip,
  a DNA fist grasping our real estate tighter and tighter.

(obsequious sequence in our standard times)
...find a new exchange rate, visit Waitanyuan, the British
consulate now a financier's club, as someone's dollar
floats on the Huangpu. Nearby they're using Joe Lovano's
saxophone to scent the air with money so that people
will want to own diamonds or Gao Xiao Wu's fat statues
and even though the names of the banks are changing
their fines are like those planes from southern China,
entering another stratosphere with ethics set exquisitely free...

(shanghArt supermarket, after Xu Zhen)
Convenience store replication
with a cashier selling to no-one.
Deep fears of overproduction
start here and continue now even
Hypercolor Buddha can't save you.
So open every packet, devour
the emptiness like manufactured
Zen in a shelf-stacked reality.

(self-service and the gift of departure)
On the day I tell my grandmother
that I will visit Guangzhou and Kaiping
she says, 'Why would you want to go there?
Why not Taiwan instead? It's richer.'
Hers is a multiple-choice illusion of
dream threads tying us back to places
that are not our own. But this is also every
location right? we're all just passing through, etc.

(tag)
New credit art rating
the post-factoried district
in any given metropolis
where graffiti is now per-
mitted   798 reasons you
will tally those sanctioned
exchanges whose echoes
paint the town red.

(old haunts)
That guy-*geist* following you around
Glenquarie shops muttering 'you eat dogs,
you eat dogs' as though invoking
an evil spirit   or a ghost-councillor
approving development applications
for donors rebuilding their imperial
guesthouses in a minecrafted
landscape, raw-materialled and serene.

(deutero-systematic perception)
At a traffic crossing
in the French concession
a peripheral injunction arrives
spirit-whispered like the oral law.
You can half hear it
over the world's constant notifications
those angel-servants delivering winds
when trucks flash past.

Tell it like it is

I believe we are in danger of being swamped
by Asians. I believe in the Holy Spirit, those wholly
Chinese ghettos, the forgiveness of sins. Surely
they're moving because no-one would want

to live beside more bloody Chinese. Come thou fount
of every resources boom payday. Look, the data's fairly
uncertain because the markets haven't factored in nearly
enough risk. House prices are high, to be blunt,

because of all these Dragon investors. Fail rates
indicate that many international students just cheat,
and they're taking places from my Sandra and your Jack.

Just think about it. If no one in Sydney ever assimilates,
what were the ANZACs even fighting for? So keep
up the pressure and we'll soon take this country back.

Blend

(precious petals)
Metal railings shepherding people
into the thrilling strands of their new careers
deciphered from certain patterns of traffic and differentiated
analytics.   This chain restaurant mitosis is just
career advice reformatted into a non-demotic script
like an infinite number of streaming devices set to shuffle.
We are promised the graceful sonar of contentedness
and the feeling will arrive on time (it must).

(bribe not accepted)
Asiatic static and you're double
voicing the exact moment
a motorcycle rider rearranges
his cargo on this fine day where
law enforcement won't forget
the rules, the uniformed officer's
mouth a straight line like a newly
opened highway in Guizhou province.

(ignorance and the decibel child)
Somehow your grandmother is babysitting
and the volume on the video of her Cantonese opera
is always-and-already increasing. But every time you
leave your bed your grandmother pretends
that she doesn't even know how the remote works,
so you turn the TV down and then return to your room,
waiting for those levels to rise again, for the windows
to shake because of construction sites in far-off cities.

(lion dance practice)
Outside the Ren Wei ancestral temple
drumbeats are shaking Guangzhou
causing small waves to ripple across Liwan Lake
causing tremors in lanes of traffic
causing nightmares for a sleeping child in Haizhu district,
as a dragon with closed eyes
pursues him across empty streets.
Run little one. Run until morning.

(riot in the talkback arcade lounge room)
Sieve dimensions
set in error mean
centuries of gold-
panning become
nothing more than
awkward gold-
farming waste-of-
time occupations.

(before the law)
How many of these skyscrapers
are made from bits of not my land,
are swaying like bruised reeds?
Pitchbend your organisational theories
because the scale of this array means
you can no longer facilitate those processes
with commitments or emergent feedback,
even if the buildings snare fog and these bland words.

(chromatic)
My mother is losing her Cantonese. She sits
on a stool in our backyard, as my father
dyes her hair black again, scalp foaming
like the edges of another oil-spilled sea.
Over dinner I will take a photo of my grandmother
and my mother, their two half-smiles settling
alongside one another, a white/black-haired reversal,
silent line of non-symmetry intuited through a screen.

(afterimage when you can't look directly at the sun)
The Chikan backstreet effect is dementia-chic,
i.e. those ornate balconies slowly corroding
under your short-film sepia glare or
the residue of last century's industrial advances.
And language is already straining this experience
like a half-hearted net in a swiftly flowing river,
catching the large stuff, bringing it fresh
to the table, but letting too much slide by.

The benefits of civic living

(redacted action plan)
There's too little self-regard to waste
    when every 'is' becomes an 'ought'
        when Starbucks becomes a death angel
            overlooking Tiananmen square.
Hey, it's just that kind of lazy observation
which ruins art for the rest of us.
Exhibit A: mosquito fade-out soundtrack.
Exhibit B: branch of hyssop like a muted guitar part.

(low occupancy's hidden division)
New South China Mall calls
out to you in its forlorn emptiness
from somewhere across the map
and so you zoom out (two fingers),
estimate new distances in the world's app,
those space-timed abstractions
now that roads are just lines of blank verse
waiting for someone to streetview them to life.

(my great-grandmother breaks her arm and is diagnosed with cancer)
This occurs only because she joyously farewells
our family after a visit to Randwick. Trying to cross
a low wall she loses balance, and gravity's
own eagerness hugs my great-grandmother against
the cracked pavement. Then hospital scans
start showing us more than we can bear, while
back at the racecourse busses multiply
like cells dividing with tricks of cruel light.

(on first looking at a Shanghai real estate agency)
With the Sydney market opening up like a Westfields boomgate
I try to envisage all those houses my grandmother bought
and quick-flipped, folding equity into terraced doorways
or Randwick apartment blocks or sandstone freestanders
accruing value even alongside our stories of loss. What
does it profit a woman or man here, buying off the plan
in this far-off city, where each concession runs backwards
touching my spine with dark rumours of capital gain?

(acknowledge your outsources)
When we all line up for Foxconn jobs
I remember that I have left
my other self, the one from the multiverse,
in Shanghai World of Books. He is (I am) apparently
still stuck on floor seven watching some guy
perfecting his comb-over in the store's mirrored walls.
Note that a multiplicity of angles is helpful here, like the
mise-en-abyme contagion of an interviewer's smile.

(habeas corpus, or achievement unlocked)
Isn't it the case, dr insert name, that
the climax of deracinated privilege
means you are just selectively retrieving
the past, working out what to discard
or pocket when you sense you've actually
gotta keep everything to save anything...
plastic bags, jars of teeth, names of villages,
full beer bottles, taut and ready to explode?

(ad-venture)
Efficiency dividend the shortcut
that doesn't pay off, losing one self
you're out of data in a new-old city,
building site scaffolding like bamboo
hashtags camped around a high-rise.
The evangelical in you wants a sign,
but there are heaps of them covering
everything and whatever he called it that was its name.

(cut common time)
Where the mattress hardens, where the oil
leaps from the fryer and strikes your wrist
like an admonition,   you're surprised by sheer
anger, by those old hurts still carried around
like keys to houses one can no longer inhabit.
Now turn to scene seven
                    meaning past the now¬yet
and into those phrases you'll sing with the nations.

Filling out a Form

What will you write in the space? Last
time you left it blank, or just put, 'Aust-
tralian.' That's the way things get glossed
in multicultures like ours, right? Classed

as mashed-potato-fried-rice-vigour-half-caste
you won't symbolise the best of what
the country's categories allow (not
that you care). And yet, here, when asked

to fill in 'ethnicity' you find yourself hesitating,
as though stranded atop the median strip
of John St, Cabra, passed by streams of traffic.

At home, cunning chicken thighs are marinating
in ricewine vinegar, dark soy, ginger, garlic,
and star anise (NB: not all futures are this aromatic).

So much that we have lost and
cannot hope to regain

(transcendental etude)
In Shanghai, opposite the People's Park, a girl
begins to cross the road and inexplicably her
smartphone leaps from her hand as though
it were a fish in a small market stall.
People are disturbed, somebody cries out in anguish,
and when she picks up the phone from the pavement
its screen is beautifully shattered with new lines
like the metro map you are handed as you walk away.

(a dream about Matthew 25)
You're scrabbling to get your talent back from the ground
but it has been shipped off and you are left breathing in
coal dust, knowing that the Chinese government has
just allowed its first solar company to fail.
Will you make my joy complete by walking through a mall
where Kenny G plays an infinite arrangement
of 'Jesu, Joy of Man's Desiring' and market forces
sing the middle class into existence?

(minor doses)

Your spaces, child-mother, those gaps in
a Surry Hills house that seemed to
close even before you opened them, a
mind harried by the things that moth and
rust will expose. Now clear the
path, sweep it in the New Canton if
you can bear this return. See it
for yourself and test its weak edges.

(seven citystatements)

One: a single source for ten thousand things.
Two: registers at supermarkets faking your receipts.
Three: filial love as a fungible commodity.
Four and five: two families quietly eating
one another in their small businesses dealings.
Six: memories of clear sunlight glinting
from a commuter's new laptop screen.
Seven: tollroad propaganda winning you back.

(house church in three or four locations)
Your second fear is to be left carrying shopping bags
in an empty square.
Back on the Bund a solitary worker re-inks the names
of corporate sponsors onto the People's Heroes' Monument.
Some mornings you imagine a building that has
not yet been marked for demolition because a family
prays and holds back progress with scarred hearts
and arms.

(spring meditation on Du Fu's autumn meditations number eight)
Two immortal companions share a Mercedes
as evening approaches Shanghai,
and when their vehicle passes Yuyuan gardens
shadows float over rebuilt walls
causing vendors look up with concern.
Surely you sense these two even now, don't you,
when the lights on Weihai road flicker?
Stay calm. Predict a surplus. Everything is gain.

(carrying error)
Demonstrate your newly discovered aesthetic with
a Paul Frank towel hanging from a fusebox
accidentally videoed by a lost visitor.
The alleyway seems to narrow
at this particular point:
record is now stop
stop is now record
lucky monkey.

(expect great things)
Diatonic happiness, who could ask for anything more?
But sometimes you freeze with the title screen
when the cover art doesn't match the blurb
which doesn't match the disc which doesn't match
your expectations of the filmed encounter.
Because you think everyone thinks of you this way,
all blended circumstance, all faux-eastwest style
(that's only on bad days, not reimaged reimagined days).

Stick with your group

(incarnate suburb)
The quarried stone body of the city
is not your body   for the paths
of Beijing's citizens   are
beyond tracing out.   You remember
being younger, learning about   China
from a returned church missionary,
copying his measured facts onto a piece of white
cardboard,   reading the country back into yourself.

(Parkview Green secret gallery)
Prosperous geometry in the Asian Century
    with Escher's mall escalators like swapped
        derivatives showing us levels that are as
            inaccessible as the stars we must believe in
                through the Beijing mist yet we do find Stella
                    McCartney and those Fangcaodi sculptures blessing
                        every transaction and we do find this moment
                            in a serrated cathedral that allegorises nothing.

(distant sister)
The murmur of shoppers becomes a river that has long disappeared
and we are both silently reading poems as the food grows cold
and I imagine our mothers telling us that we must now eat
and in one afternoon this city of dust has become like a
flame held too close to my skin and I feel it peeling me back
exposing my heartbeat like a huge mechanical sea turtle.
And later, when you quietly begin to sing, the streets stretch out
along mythic meridians and suddenly I'm afraid to walk them alone.

(even chance, or why you find it difficult to speak with people in a lift)
Peaceful evil
turbo-dieselling
consumer sentiment
with your dumb tongue
like that folding bicycle
your uncle brought
back from Taiwan
in his decade of tricks and risk.

(glossolalia)
Sometimes I discover myself by
broadening the Aussie accent
in particular locations, e.g. Hutong bars
where the American law students
regroup before New York swallows
them whole again. Back home this helps me blend
in, when I'm in Australian country towns where
I'm meant to live and move and have my being.

(making a man)
You try to remix every belt in the belt shop
then, suit suit suit, tie tie tie, plastic wrapping
you can dispose of yourself, along with that
jacket you bought just to have a chance of fit-
ing in. But size means nothing here, a history
presses into your shoulders, and the young
assistant's hands reach around your throat
tightening sale time love overstock delight.

(move to consumption)
Listen to this old Beijing woman who walks
Xuanwumenwai avenue, applauding the traffic
and those groups of people kicking a shuttlecock
in front of the Omega store where no one is
buying anything.   O sing of clean bones
in the broken capital where the thick atmosphere
arcs over you like a broad and elegant flight-path
or the promise of a perfect supply chain.

(fifth circle or a day in another person's person)
        Ring roads Beijing the company with
thirty office staff all called Ricky Wong.
        The system names its vehicles auspiciously,
the fleet kept up to date by e-calendar
        reminders chirping at key moments, say,
4am when the sky just forgets its pollution
        or tolerates a microsleep between jobs.
Two breaths before the long shift begins.

Artistic Licenses

Incidents you just need to forget about for a while:
your father gets a comment about mail order brides,
your brother goes for a run around leafy St Ives,
and is yelled at by a tradie mimicking 'Gangnam Style'

dance moves with hi-vis humour. Meanwhile, a rival-
ry in your creative writing class ends with two guys
joking about Asians eating cats. Your mother cries
after being abused in the street. She reads the Bible

in church and gets complimented on her
ability to speak English. Your overseas relations
joke about Chinese migrant workers drowning

off the coast of Morecambe ('What's for dinner?'
said the shark). You rethink your motivations
for writing. You catch yourself frowning.

Blank face double vision

(where are you really from?)
Mechanically looping this question
through the speakers at Beijing Workers'
Stadium, the concrete reverberates like
holes in your starting line-up. And there's
just this one guy cheering for the Aussie
team, which loses after playing dirty
and the Guoan fans light flares, smoke
cigarettes and yell *sha bi* into the night.

(self-justification)
Every stupid thing has a story
that ties it back to the house.
Words follow me outside,
threaten quiet atrocities.
After a while I stop
listening to outro tracks,
the security door locking on its own,
my body leaving to fill the sixth dumpster.

(hoards)
One morning a man rides a bicycle down a hutong
    and at the end of the alley a Buick GL8 snorts and rises
        like a water buffalo in a rice paddy. Then you glance
            sideways for touristic reasons and find your gaze
        caught by a workshop that is filled with clothes
    and striped bags, and for less than a second this is
your grandmother's brimming house in Ashfield,
and when you look down at your hands they won't stop shaking.

(eco-leisure company building the impossible)
Creation's precious myths
open out when another golf course
appears alongside a housing estate,
the sounds of sprinklers
on non-existent greens
stitching water into the cool evening air.
Technically no-one will ever tee off,
though who can see over these artificial hills?

(learning the ABC)
My mother takes me aside, tells me of the time
her primary school almost made her dux.
Then at the last minute the test got replaced
by something about proverbs and sayings.
    A stitch in time saves…
    The early bird gets the…
This forty-degree day lacerates all wisdom,
sends our dreams spiralling from classroom windows.

(rational sensible limits)
Everyone's selling political souvenirs like they're
subsidised, e.g. the driver's ringtone set to Chinese
national anthem or the white umbilical cord
connecting a smartphone with its battery pack.
Toward dusk, when the sky is passport blue,
you return via the National Performing Arts Centre,
its vast half-egg reflected in the stirring water, the wind
smashing cold miracles into Beijing's atmosphere.

(centred)
Two billion reasons for insignificance:
your suspicious history, your unpronounceable name,
eyes and the split condition like a racist delta
with tributaries drying up, or a series of overlaid characters
now disappearing one by one due to explicable drought.
And when your grandmother reads aloud, traces her fingers
over the engravings at Rookwood cemetery, her words erect
a magnificent pavilion, endowing the future with promise.

(sabbath)
Under the Great Wall I will rest in an abandoned
farmhouse, just two rooms collapsing slowly
into the clear cold, single bricks falling from the roofline.
It will be spring, but with some ponds still frozen.
My hands will forget themselves, three goats will
scamper past, and then my breath will surprise me,
like a hare bursting through coarse undergrowth
startling itself with the suddenness of exposure.

Almost there

(Quanjude audience of the just)
A distributive recitative,
a Beijing duck value state-
ment or a new sect-
ion always played *colla voce*.
Hail those beast seas and their waves
cutting into the Hainan coast-
line, crisp skin like the edges
of a nation warmed globally.

(why we cannot invent the past)
There is a picture of my uncle posing with my great-grandparents
as though he were their son. It rests on a shelf next to my
grandmother,
as she sighs and spits out forgiveness like loose sunflower seeds.
In the winter, after her house has been cleaned, after my father
has pressed himself under the floorboards and reconstructed old
foundations,
my uncle will move in. Strange that it has come to this last pairing,
in that stage of life where the brush turns sideways
and the black line narrows in the emphysemic light.

(non-sober judgement)
You're anxious that each new insight is just
self-surveillance missing/hitting its mark,
the sky-like mirror in a nightclub bathroom
in Chaoyang district.   Before the literary festival
you ask six different people to take your photo
as you hold yourself inside a discarded
picture frame and each rejection makes you
stronger, a telemarketer with implacable spirit.

(complicit empire)
Order of operations in the current climate.
Feigned sleep and the political uses of Confucianism.
A thousand crane arms like automated chopsticks
setting down fragments of shell and bone.
These hydraulic statements of fact are
press-released to make my joy complete:
wanting only what can be produced
producing only what can be wanted.

(failed to do)
Futile trips down souvenir streets always accentuate
those distances between me and a brutal century.
So what can I gather on this final day?
And what have you gathered in your lifetime?
How did the landscape whisper between bombings?
White breath sifts particulates from the air,
the wind grips my arm, and I'm imagining your hands
picking their way through our growing mountain of debris.

(this will not occur)
My lines of caffeinated searching
bringing it all together, *stretto* charm.
A last minute reunion with lost relatives,
subject, answer and countersubject,
earnest as a Tai-pop keychange
or the predawn repetitions of Bach
with joints cracking in the cold,
my hands memorising another coda.

(white white)
Grandmother, when you sing 'Jesus loves me' in Cantonese
I don't think I should write any more. We take you out
for dinner and you lean on your frame next to Liverpool Road,
where the path's gentle gradient tips the breath from your lips.
You tell me you are scared that the window behind you might shatter.
On the other side of its glass we glimpse a relative who has died.
I have been teaching my sons to call you *Bak Bak* and now we hear
their small voices greeting the moon as it rises above a church spire.

Notes

p. 3 (a future for each object):

Title taken from a quote from Wu Hung's book *Waste Not*, a set of writings and notes accompanying the art installation of the same name by Song Dong and Zhao Xiangyuan.

p. 9 (overseas Chinese are the mother of revolution):

Title taken from a quote by Sun Yat-sen.

p. 10 (in youth mode, you are infinite):

Title taken from K-HOLE's trend report *Youth Mode: A Report on Freedom*. 'Start acting basic' is also taken from this trend report.

p. 23 (as for me):

The lines '[we] can connect nothing/ with nothing' taken from T.S. Eliot's *The Waste Land*.

p. 32 ('11 arrested for leaking exam questions'):

Title taken from a *China Daily* headline.

p. 38 (shanghArt supermarket, after Xu Zhen):

Responds to Xu Zhen's installation *shanghArt supermarket* which is a recreation of a fully stocked convenience store but with all the product packages empty.

p. 47 (before the law):

Title taken from a parable by Franz Kafka (and an essay by Jacques Derrida responding to it).

p. 61 (spring meditation on autumn meditations number eight):

'Autumn Meditations Number Eight' is a poem by Du Fu.

p. 62 (expect great things):

Title taken from a quote by William Carey, missionary to India.

Acknowledgements

Parts of this volume were written with the aid of an Australia Council for the Arts, Emerging Writers' Grant whilst on sabbatical from Charles Sturt University. Poems from the book have appeared in *Axon, The Best Australian Poems 2016, Cha, Kitaab, Mascara Literary Review, Once Wild: The Newcastle Poetry Prize Anthology 2014, Pencilled In, St Mark's Review, Underneath: The University of Canberra Vice-Chancellor's International Poetry Prize 2015.* Warm and unreserved thanks to Bo Fei, Yanting Wu, Mai Yu, He Yan, Diane Grady, Rosalyn Shih, David Gilbey, Alex Segal, Mark Macleod, Seumas Macdonald, Mohammed Ahmad, Luke Carman, Felicity Castagna, Fiona Wright, Emily Stewart and Ivor Indyk. Much love and thanks to my precious family, Corinne, Hamish, Oliver, and Inara.

The Giramondo Publishing Company acknowledges the support of Western Sydney University in the implementation of its book publishing program.